Published By Adam Gilbin

@ Juan Burke

Alkaline Diet: Secret to Vibrant Living on Whole Food Diet, and Nourishing Alkaline Recipes for a Healthier You

All Right RESERVED

ISBN 978-87-94477-72-7

TABLE OF CONTENTS

Meal Recipe Plan 1

Quinoa And Vegetable Stir 2

Lentil Soup 3

Alkaline Spinach Salad 5

Alkaline Veggie Wrap 6

Alkaline Roasted Vegetables, ... 7

Red Lentil And Kale Soup 8

Quinoa 10

Blueberry Omega Morning Blast 13

Cucumber Lavender Water. 15

Strawberry Quinoa Breakfast 16

Almond Butter Crunch Berry Smoothie 18

Quinoa Morning Porridge 19

Apple And Almond Butter Oats 20

Quinoa Burrito Bowl 22

Black Pepper To Taste 24

Almond Butter And Banana Sandwich 26

- Alkaline Green Smoothie 27
- Quinoa Salad With Chickpeas 28
- Baked Salmon With Steamed Asparagus 30
- Green Salad With Avocado 32
- Baked Salmon With Steamed Asparagus 34
- Sweet Potato And Chickpea Curry 36
- Breakfast Smoothie 38
- Grilled Lemon Herb Chicken 40
- Vanilla And Spelt Pancakes 42
- Green Breakfast Smoothie 43
- Pesto-Topped Alkaline Zucchini Noodles 45
- Alkaline Roasted Cauliflower Bowl (Recipe 13) 47
- Alkaline Cabbage And Carrot Slaw (Recipe 14) 49
- Chia Seed Alkaline Pudding 51
- Gazpacho With Alkaline Cucumber 53
- Alkaline Berry Parfait (Recipe 20) 55
- Raw Chili 57
- Blackberry Smoothie 59

- Savory Avocado Wrap 60
- Onion And Pepper Masala 62
- Cauliflower Gnocchi 64
- Cole Slaw With Avocado Dressing 67
- Fresh Garden Vegetable Salad 68
- Broccoli Salad With Tofu 70
- Avocado Salad With Wild Garlic 72
- Mediterranean Salad 74
- Prepare The Salad Dressing: 76
- Quick & Easy Salad 77
- Meal Recipe Plan 78
- Quinoa And Vegetable Stir 79
- Lentil Soup 80
- Alkaline Spinach Salad 82
- Alkaline Veggie Wrap 83
- Alkaline Roasted Vegetables, ... 84
- Red Lentil And Kale Soup 85
- Quinoa 87

- Blueberry Omega Morning Blast 90
- Cucumber Lavender Water. 92
- Strawberry Quinoa Breakfast 93
- Almond Butter Crunch Berry Smoothie 95
- Quinoa Morning Porridge 96
- Apple And Almond Butter Oats 97
- Quinoa Burrito Bowl 99
- Black Pepper To Taste 101
- Almond Butter And Banana Sandwich 103
- Alkaline Green Smoothie 104
- Quinoa Salad With Chickpeas 105
- Baked Salmon With Steamed Asparagus 107
- Green Salad With Avocado 109
- Baked Salmon With Steamed Asparagus 111
- Sweet Potato And Chickpea Curry 113
- Breakfast Smoothie 115
- Grilled Lemon Herb Chicken 117
- Vanilla And Spelt Pancakes 119

- Green Breakfast Smoothie 121
- Tropical Vegetable And Fruit Mix 123
- Pineapple And Coconut Smoothie 124
- Additional Vegetables For Broth 125
- Sesame Flavored Broccoli Salad 127
- Sweet Potato And Lentil Bowl 128
- Alkaline Avocado And Cucumber Salad (Recipe 10) 129
- Stuffed Bell Peppers 130
- Pesto-Topped Alkaline Zucchini Noodles 132

Meal Recipe Plan

INGREDIENTS:

- 12 an avocado
- Half a lemon, juiced
- 1 chopped and cored green apple
- Spinach, 1 cup
- Half a cucumber
- Coconut water, 1 cup

Directions:

1. All INGREDIENTS: should be smoothly combined.
2. As a hydrating and alkalizing breakfast smoothie.

Quinoa And Vegetable Stir

INGREDIENTS:

- cooked quinoa, 1 cup
- 1 cup of mixed vegetables, including carrots, broccoli, bell peppers, and snap peas
- Olive oil, two tablespoons
- 1 tablespoon soy sauce or tamari
- 1 teaspoon of ginger, grated
- Sesame seeds, 1 teaspoon

Directions:

1. In a pan, heat the olive oil.
2. Ginger that has been grated should be included. till somewhat tender, stir-fry.
3. Add tamari and cooked quinoa. Mix thoroughly.
4. Sesame seeds can be added before serving.

Lentil Soup

INGREDIENTS:

- 2 minced garlic cloves
- Six cups of vegetable stock
- Turmeric, 1 teaspoon
- 1/9 cup cumin
- Pepper and salt as desired
- Dried green lentils, 1 cup
- One sliced onion
- 2 sliced carrots
- 2 chopped celery stalks
- Garnishing with fresh parsley

Directions:

1. In a pot, sauté celery, carrots, and onion until tender.

2. Add the cumin, turmeric, and garlic. For one minute, cook.
3. Include vegetable broth and lentils. Till lentils are cooked, simmer.
4. Add salt and pepper to taste.
5. Before serving, garnish with fresh parsley.

Alkaline Spinach Salad

INGREDIENTS:

- 1 sliced red bell pepper
- 1/4 of a thinly sliced red onion
- 30 grams of pumpkin seeds
- Tahini-lemon dressing
- 4 cups of young spinach
- Sliced cucumber, one

Directions:

1. Salad bowl with baby spinach in it.
2. Slices of red onion, red bell pepper, and cucumber should be placed on top.
3. Pumpkin seeds should be added to the salad.
4. Add a lemon-tahini dressing drizzle.

Alkaline Veggie Wrap

INGREDIENTS:

- Sliced red bell pepper, half
- Sliced cucumbers, 1/4
- Sprouts (of broccoli or alfalfa)
- Pepper and salt as desired
- One whole-wheat wrap
- 50 ml of hummus
- 1 cup of mixed greens (arugula, kale, and spinach)
- Sliced avocado, half

Directions:

1. Wrapped in hummus, of course.
2. Add sprouts, red bell pepper, cucumber, avocado, and mixed greens on a plate.
3. Add salt and pepper to taste.
4. Cut the wrap in half after rolling it up.

Alkaline Roasted Vegetables,

INGREDIENTS:

- 1 teaspoon dried oregano, thyme, and rosemary
- pepper and salt as desired
- 2 cups of mixed veggies, including carrots, bell peppers, cauliflower, and zucchini
- Olive oil, two tablespoons

Directions:

1. Set the oven's temperature to 400°F (200°C).
2. Combine olive oil, dried herbs, salt, and pepper with the mixed veggies.
3. Vegetables are spread out on a baking pan.
4. Roast for 20 to 25 minutes, or until vegetables are soft and gently browned.

Red Lentil And Kale Soup

INGREDIENTS:

- 2 stalks of celery, chopped
- 1 bunch of kale, cut into ribbons
- 6 cups of vegetable broth
- 1 ½ cup red lentils, rinsed
- 1 tablespoon coconut oil
- 1 medium onion, finely chopped
- 4 garlic cloves, minced
- 2 large carrots, chopped
- Salt and pepper to taste

Directios:

1. Heat the oil in a large pot over medium heat. Add the onion and sauté until translucent – 3-5 minutes.

2. Add the garlic, carrots, celery and kale and sauté for 2-3 minutes. Add the broth, lentils, salt and pepper.
3. Cook on medium-low heat until lentils are tender, 20 minutesuinoa Stuffed Tomatoes

Quinoa

INGREDIENTS:

- 1 can cannellini beans (i use eden organics, thoroughly rinsed and drained)
- 3 tbsp. Basil, julienned (thin strips)
- 2 tsp. Coconut oil
- 2 cups filtered water
- Sea salt (celtic grey sea salt, himalayan, or redmond real salt)
- 1 cup quinoa
- 4 medium tomatoes
- 3 cups baby spinach
- 2 cloves of garlic, minced
- Black pepper to taste

Directions:

1. Preheat oven to 375 degrees. Hollow out the tomatoes by cutting around the top of the tomato and scooping out the inside.
2. Slice a small section off the bottom of the tomato so it sits flat on the baking sheet. Sprinkle the inside of the tomatoes with some salt.
3. Cook quinoa by combining 2 cups of water with 1 cup of rinsed quinoa in a pot over high heat.
4. When the water comes to a boil, cover the pot and turn heat down to the lowest setting for 30 minutes.
5. Heat coconut oil in a pan, add garlic and brown lightly. Add beans, crush them slightly with a wooden spoon, and cook for one minute.
6. Add spinach and cook until wilted. Add basil. Season with sea salt and pepper.

7. Mix spinach mixture with quinoa. Divide the filling among the tomatoes. Place on a baking sheet lined with parchment paper.
8. Add a little water to the bottom of the baking sheet (4 tbsp. is plenty). Bake for 15-20 minutes at 375 degrees.

Blueberry Omega Morning Blast

INGREDIENTS:

- 1 Tbsp. chia
- 1 Tbsp. ground flaxseed
- 1 Tbsp. hemp seed powder
- 1 Tbsp. coconut oil
- 1 cup coconut milk
- 1 large handful of spinach
- ½ cup blueberries
- 1 Tbsp. raw almond butter

Directions:

1. Preheat oven to 375 degrees. Hollow out the tomatoes by cutting around the top of the tomato and scooping out the inside.
2. Slice a small section off the bottom of the tomato so it sits flat on the baking sheet.

Sprinkle the inside of the tomatoes with some salt.
3. Cook quinoa by combining 2 cups of water with 1 cup of rinsed quinoa in a pot over high heat.
4. When the water comes to a boil, cover the pot and turn heat down to the lowest setting for 30 minutes.
5. Heat coconut oil in a pan, add garlic and brown lightly. Add beans, crush them slightly with a wooden spoon, and cook for one minute.
6. Add spinach and cook until wilted. Add basil. Season with sea salt and pepper.
7. Mix spinach mixture with quinoa. Divide the filling among the tomatoes. Place on a baking sheet lined with parchment paper.
8. Add a little water to the bottom of the baking sheet (4 tbsp. is plenty). Bake for 15-20 minutes at 375 degrees.

Cucumber Lavender Water.

INGREDIENTS:

- 1 teaspoon dried lavender

- 1 small cucumber, thinly sliced

- 8 cups filtered water

DIRECTIONS:

1. Combine all INGREDIENTS: in a pitcher and refrigerate for up to 12 hours to allow water to infuse.
2. Watermelon Mint Infused Water

Strawberry Quinoa Breakfast

INGREDIENTS:

- 2 tbsp. unsweetened shredded coconut flakes
- 5 tbsp. chia seeds
- 2 tbsp. almond pieces
- 1 cup cooked quinoa
- 2 pitted dates
- 1 ½ cup almond, coconut or hemp milk
- ½ cup quartered strawberries + 4 sliced strawberries

Directions:

1. Cook quinoa the night before and prepare the chia by blending almond milk with strawberries and 2 dates.
2. Blend until smooth, and then pour into a jar where you will add the chia seeds. Mix them as well as you can and then refrigerate.

3. Keep in mind that you need to put the lid on before refrigerating. In the morning before eating, place them all in a bowl and then add the quinoa and chia in.
4. Add almonds, strawberry slices, and shredded coconut.

Almond Butter Crunch Berry Smoothie

INGREDIENTS:

- 1 cup of any of the following (frozen mixed berries, strawberries or grapes)
- 1 tbsp. chia
- 4 tbsp. raw almond butter
- 2 cups fresh spinach
- 1 banana (peeled and frozen)
- 2 cups almond milk, unsweetened

Directions:

1. Blend in spinach with the almond milk. Add the remaining INGREDIENTS: in except the chia and then puree until smooth.
2. When it is smooth, add the chia and blend again at a very low speed. Let sit for a few minutes for the chia seeds to expand and then drink.

Quinoa Morning Porridge

INGREDIENTS:

- 1 tsp. chia seeds
- 1 tsp. hemp seeds
- ½ cup rinsed quinoa
- 1 15 oz. can of coconut milk
- 1 tsp. cinnamon

Directions:

1. Get all the INGREDIENTS: except hemp seeds and let them cook on the stove. Let them simmer for ten to fifteen minutes until all the liquid is absorbed.
2. When is it prepared, sprinkle it with hemp seeds to bring it all together as a very special little porridge.

Apple And Almond Butter Oats

INGREDIENTS:

- 1/3 cup raw almond butter
- 1 tsp. cinnamon
- 1 cup grated green apple
- 1 ½ cups coconut milk
- 2 cups gluten-free oats

Directions:

1. Take the oats and put them in a bowl. Add in coconut milk and almond butter to mix them all together.
2. When they are mixed, cover the bowl with a lid or plastic wrap and refrigerate. You will need to leave this in the refrigerator overnight, so it is better to prepare it the last night.
3. If the oats get too thick, though, you may add some extra coconut milk to even it out.

Garnish it with cinnamon powder before eating.

Quinoa Burrito Bowl

INGREDIENTS:

- 4 garlic cloves, minced

- 1 heaping tsp. cumin

- 2 avocados, sliced

- 2 limes, fresh juiced

- 1 cup quinoa (or brown rice)

- 4 green onions (scallions), sliced

- 2 15-oz cans of black or adzuki beans

- a small handful of cilantros, chopped

DIRECTIONS:

1. Cook the quinoa or rice (whichever you choose) with warm beans on a light flame. Stir it and add lime juice, onions, garlic, and cumin and then let the flavors

combine for ten to fifteen minutes. When the rice is finished, serve in separate bowls after being topped with beans, avocado, cilantro, and any other garnishing you may like.

Black Pepper To Taste

INGREDIENTS:

- ½ cup kelp noodles, soaked and drained
- 1/3 cup cherry tomatoes, halved
- 2 tbsp. hemp seeds
- 3 cups kale, chopped
- ½ cup broccoli florets, chopped
- ½ zucchini (make noodles with a pasta roller)

Directions:

1. Flash steam the broccoli with kale for four minutes and then set it aside.
2. Mix the noodles you have rolled from zucchini and toss them with a serving of smoked avocado cumin dressing that you have prepared.
3. Add the cherry tomatoes and then toss the mixture. If preferred, drizzle the salad with

lemon tahini dressing and top it off with the dressed noodles.
4. Sprinkle the entire dish with hem seeds and enjoy.

Almond Butter And Banana Sandwich

INGREDIENTS:

- 1 ripe banana, sliced
- Honey for drizzling
- 2 slices whole-grain bread
- 2 tablespoons almond butter

Directions:

1. Spread almond butter evenly on one slice of bread.
2. Lay banana slices on top of the almond butter.
3. Drizzle honey over the bananas if desired.
4. Top with the second slice of bread.
5. Press the sandwich together gently.
6. Slice in half diagonally if you prefer.

Alkaline Green Smoothie

INGREDIENTS:

- 1 cup almond milk (alkaline)
- 1/2 lemon, juiced (alkaline)
- 1 teaspoon honey (acidic, use sparingly)
- 1 cup spinach (alkaline)
- 1 banana (alkaline)
- 1/2 avocado (alkaline)
- 1 tablespoon almond butter (alkaline)

Directions:

1. Blend all INGREDIENTS: until smooth.
2. Add honey if desired for sweetness (use sparingly).

Quinoa Salad With Chickpeas

INGREDIENTS:

- 1/4 cup cherry tomatoes (alkaline)

- 1/4 cucumber (alkaline)

- 2 tablespoons olive oil (alkaline)

- 1 tablespoon lemon juice (alkaline)

- Salt and pepper to taste (use sparingly)

- 1 cup cooked quinoa (alkaline)

- 1/2 cup chickpeas (alkaline)

- 1 cup mixed greens (alkaline)

Directions:

1. In a large bowl, combine quinoa, chickpeas, mixed greens, cherry tomatoes, and cucumber.
2. In a separate bowl, whisk together olive oil and lemon juice.

3. Drizzle the dressing over the salad and toss to combine.
4. Season with salt and pepper to taste (use sparingly).

Baked Salmon With Steamed Asparagus

INGREDIENTS:

- 1 clove garlic, minced (alkaline)
- Lemon wedges for garnish (alkaline)
- Salt and pepper to taste (use sparingly)
- 6-ounce salmon fillet (alkaline)
- 1 bunch asparagus spears (alkaline)
- 1 tablespoon olive oil (alkaline)

Directions:

1. Preheat the oven to 375°F (190°C).
2. Place the salmon fillet on a baking sheet lined with parchment paper.
3. In a small bowl, mix olive oil and minced garlic. Brush the mixture onto the salmon.
4. Season the salmon with salt and pepper to taste (use sparingly).
5. Arrange asparagus spears around the salmon.

6. Bake for 15-20 minutes or until the salmon flakes easily with a fork.
7. Serve with lemon wedges for garnish.

Green Salad With Avocado

INGREDIENTS:

- ¼ cup red onion, thinly sliced
- ¼ cup feta cheese, crumbled
- 2 tablespoons olive oil
- 1 tablespoon lemon juice
- Salt and pepper to taste
- 4 cups mixed greens (lettuce, spinach, arugula, etc.)
- 1 ripe avocado, diced
- ¼ cup cherry tomatoes, halved
- ¼ cup cucumber, sliced

Directions:

1. In a large salad bowl, combine mixed greens, diced avocado, cherry tomatoes, cucumber, red onion, and crumbled feta cheese.

2. In a small bowl, whisk together olive oil, lemon juice, salt, and pepper to create the dressing.
3. Drizzle the dressing over the salad and gently toss to coat all INGREDIENTS: evenly.
4. Serve your Green Salad with Avocado as a light and refreshing side dish or add grilled chicken or shrimp for a complete meal.

Baked Salmon With Steamed Asparagus

INGREDIENTS:

- 2 cloves garlic, minced
- 1 lemon, sliced
- Salt and pepper to taste
- Fresh dill for garnish
- 4 salmon fillets
- 1 bunch asparagus, trimmed
- 2 tablespoons olive oil

Directions:

1. Preheat the oven to 375°F (190°C).
2. Place the salmon fillets on a baking sheet lined with parchment paper.
3. Drizzle olive oil over the salmon, then sprinkle with minced garlic, salt, and pepper. Place lemon slices on top.

4. Bake for 15-20 minutes or until the salmon flakes easily with a fork.
5. While the salmon is baking, steam the asparagus until tender-crisp, about 5-7 minutes.
6. Serve the Baked Salmon with Steamed Asparagus, garnished with fresh dill and additional lemon slices if desired.

Sweet Potato And Chickpea Curry

INGREDIENTS:

- 2 tablespoons curry powder
- 1 teaspoon ground cumin
- 1 teaspoon ground coriander
- ½ teaspoon ground turmeric
- Salt and pepper to taste
- Fresh cilantro for garnish
- 2 sweet potatoes, peeled and diced
- 1 can (15 oz) chickpeas, drained and rinsed
- 1 onion, chopped
- 2 cloves garlic, minced
- 1 can (15 oz) diced tomatoes
- 1 can (15 oz) coconut milk

Directions:

1. In a large pot, heat a bit of oil over medium heat. Add chopped onion and garlic, sauté until fragrant.
2. Add diced sweet potatoes and cook for a few minutes.
3. Stir in the curry powder, ground cumin, ground coriander, ground turmeric, salt, and pepper.
4. Pour in the diced tomatoes and coconut milk. Stir well.
5. Bring to a simmer, then cover and cook for 20-25 minutes, or until sweet potatoes are tender.
6. Add chickpeas and simmer for an additional 5 minutes.
7. Serve your Sweet Potato and Chickpea Curry hot, garnished with fresh cilantro. Enjoy with rice or naan bread.

Breakfast Smoothie

INGREDIENTS:

- 1 tablespoon chia seeds
- 1 cup coconut water
- 1 teaspoon spirulina powder
- 1 tablespoon honey
- 1 cup spinach
- ½ cucumber
- ½ avocado
- 1 banana

Directions:

1. Place spinach, cucumber, avocado, banana, chia seeds, coconut water, and spirulina powder in a blender.
2. Blend until smooth.

3. Add honey for a touch of sweetness and blend again.
4. Pour into a glass and enjoy your nutritious Alkaline Breakfast Smoothie.

Grilled Lemon Herb Chicken

INGREDIENTS:

- 2 tablespoons fresh rosemary, chopped
- 2 tablespoons fresh thyme, chopped
- Salt and pepper to taste
- 2 tablespoons olive oil
- 4 boneless, skinless chicken breasts
- 2 lemons, juiced and zested
- 2 cloves garlic, minced

Directions:

1. In a bowl, combine lemon juice, lemon zest, garlic, rosemary, thyme, salt, pepper, and olive oil to create a marinade.
2. Place chicken breasts in a resealable bag and pour the marinade over them. Seal the bag and refrigerate for at least 30 minutes.
3. Preheat the grill to medium-high heat.

4. Grill the chicken for about 6-8 minutes per side or until the internal temperature reaches 165°F (74°C).
5. Serve your Grilled Lemon Herb Chicken with your choice of sides.

Vanilla And Spelt Pancakes

INGREDIENTS:

- 1 cup organic almond milk
- 1 tbsp maple syrup (you can also use alcohol-free stevia)
- 2 tbsp sunflower oil (cold and pressed)
- 11/2 tsp alcohol-free vanilla
- 1 cup light spelt flour (spelt is a non-wheat, whole grain flour)
- 2 tbsp aluminum-free baking powder
- 1/8 tsp fine grained Himalayan salt
- ¼ tsp coconut oil for the pan

Directions:

1. Mix all the dry and wet INGREDIENTS: into two different bowls. Hence, one bowl will have spelt flour, baking powder and

Himalayan salt while the other will have almond milk, sunflower oil and vanilla.

2. Mix the dry INGREDIENTS: and wet INGREDIENTS: separately and mix them together. Leave it aside for 10 minutes to allow the batter to rise. Use the coconut oil to grease the pan lightly.
3. Keep the pan on low heat and now spoon in small amounts of the batter. Allow it to cook for 2 to 3 minutes until bubbles appear on top. Then flip to cook the underside.
4. If you make extra pancakes, simply chill them in your refrigerator and pop them in the toaster the next day!

Green Breakfast Smoothie

INGREDIENTS:

- 1 ripe avocado
- 1 cup coconut water
- Juice of one lime
- 1-2 tsp Udo's oil
- 1-2 tbsp hemp seeds
- One cucumber (about 6 Ý)
- 3 torn medium sized kale leaves
- 3 stems fresh parsley
- 5 stems fresh organic mint
- 1 Ý fresh ginger
- 2-3 drops Stevia

Directions:

1. Mix all the INGREDIENTS: in your blender until smooth and delicious! (You can add a little alkalized water if you like). If you prefer the

natural sugars in the coconut, you can consider using almond milk instead.

Pesto-Topped Alkaline Zucchini Noodles

INGREDIENTS:

- 2 spiralized zucchini for the noodles
- fresh basil leaves, 1/4 cup
- fresh parsley leaves, 1/4 cup
- Pine nuts, 14 cup
- Extra virgin olive oil, 1/4 cup
- one garlic clove
- lemon juice from one
- pepper and salt as desired

Directions:

1. Combine basil, parsley, pine nuts, garlic, and lemon juice in a blender or food processor.

2. Olive oil should be added gradually while blending to achieve a smooth pesto.

3. Combine the pesto and zucchini noodles in a bowl.

4. Add salt and pepper to taste.

5. nutritive worth:

6. 250 calories

7. alkaline-rich plants and vegetables

8. healthful fats from olive oil and pine nuts are a good supply.

9. Recommendation: Use zucchini noodles as a base for this dish with an alkaline pesto.

Alkaline Roasted Cauliflower Bowl (Recipe 13)

INGREDIENTS:

- 1 small cauliflower with separated florets.
- Olive oil, two tablespoons
- Turmeric, 1 teaspoon
- 1/9 cup cumin
- Paprika, half a teaspoon
- pepper and salt as desired
- cooked quinoa, 1 cup
- 14 cup finely minced fresh parsley
- Tahini-lemon dressing

Directions:

1. Set the oven's temperature to 400°F (200°C).

2. Cauliflower florets should be mixed with olive oil, salt, pepper, turmeric, cumin, and paprika.
3. Roast cauliflower for 25 to 30 minutes after spreading it out on a baking sheet.
4. Combine cooked quinoa, roasted cauliflower, and parsley in a bowl.
5. Add a lemon-tahini dressing drizzle.
6. nutritive worth:
7. 300 calories
8. abundant in alkalizing foods and spices
9. Quinoa is a good source of protein.
10. Having cauliflower in this tasty bowl adds heft and nutrients.

Alkaline Cabbage And Carrot Slaw (Recipe 14)

INGREDIENTS:

- 2 cups of purple or green cabbage, shredded
- 1 cup of carrots, shredded
- 14 cup finely minced fresh cilantro
- apple cider vinegar, 2 tablespoons
- Extra virgin olive oil, 1 tablespoon
- Dijon mustard, 1 teaspoon
- pepper and salt as desired

Directions:

1. Shredded cabbage, carrots, and cilantro are combined in a bowl.

2. Shake apple cider vinegar, olive oil, Dijon mustard, salt, and pepper in a small jar.

3. The slaw will be combined after the dressing has been added.

4. nutritive worth:

5. 150 calories

6. rich in fresh herbs and alkalizing vegetables

7. a good source of antioxidants and vitamins

8. Advice: The base of this slaw is made of crunchy and colorful cabbage and carrots.

Chia Seed Alkaline Pudding

INGREDIENTS:

- Chia seeds, 2 tablespoons
- 1 cup of your choice of milk, such as almond milk
- One-half teaspoon of vanilla extract
- maple syrup, 1 tbsp
- Fresh berries as a garnish

Directions:

1. Chia seeds, almond milk, maple syrup, and vanilla essence should all be combined in a bowl.
2. **To help the chia seeds absorb the liquid, stir** thoroughly and put the mixture in the fridge overnight.

3. Stir the chia mixture thoroughly in the morning.Serve with fresh berries on top.
4. nutritive worth:150 calories rich in antioxidants and plant-based omega-3s
5. Chia seeds are a good source of calcium.
6. Recommendation: Chia seeds are a nutritious and alkaline breakfast alternative.

Gazpacho With Alkaline Cucumber

INGREDIENTS:

- 2 chopped and peeled cucumbers
- 1 chopped red bell pepper
- Red onion, cut into 1/4
- 2 minced garlic cloves
- fresh basil leaves, 1/4 cup
- apple cider vinegar, 2 tablespoons
- Olive oil, extra virgin, two tablespoons
- pepper and salt as desired

Directions:

1. Cucumbers, red bell pepper, red onion, garlic, basil, apple cider vinegar, extra virgin olive oil, salt, and pepper should all be combined in a blender.

2. Until smooth, blend.

3. Before serving, let the food cool for at least an hour in the refrigerator.

Alkaline Berry Parfait (Recipe 20)

INGREDIENTS:

- 1 cup plain coconut yogurt (or any other yogurt made from plants)
- Berry mixture of blueberries, strawberries, and raspberries, 1/2 cup
- 2 tablespoons of almonds, choppe
- Chia seeds, one tablespoon
- 1 teaspoon of maple syrup or honey

Directions:

1. Layer coconut yogurt, mixed berries, almonds, and chia seeds in a glass or bowl.

2. Add a drizzle of maple syrup or honey.

3. Layers should be repeated until all components are used.

4. nutritive worth:

5. 250 calories

6. rich in plant-based omega-3s and antioxidants

7. Coconut yogurt is a good source of calcium.

are essential for a healthy alkaline diet. Before making any big dietary changes, always get medical advice.

Raw Chili

INGREDIENTS:

- 1 tomato (large)
- Sun Dried Tomatoes6 sundried tomatoes
- 2 tbsp. garlic (finely chopped)
- ½ red bell pepper
- ¼ to ½ yellow squash
- ¼ yellow onion, chopped
- 2 tbsp. olive oil
- 1 tbsp. chili powder
- 1 tsp. cumin
- ½ tsp. sea salt (Celtic grey, Himalayan, Redmond Real Salt)
- Optional: add 1 tsp. of Braggs Liquid Aminos

DIRECTIONS:

1. Place all INGREDIENTS: in the food processor with the "S" blade, pulse a few times first to chop INGREDIENTS:, and then switch to blend in the food processor to obtain desired consistency.
2. You can eat this right away, but my preference is to let sit for an hour before you serve to let all of the spices mesh together.

Blackberry Smoothie

INGREDIENTS:

- 1 ½ cups coconut milk (or almond or hemp), unsweetened
- 1 cup blackberries (frozen)
- ½ cup strawberries (frozen)
- 1 large bunch of kale
- 1 lime, fresh juiced
- 2 tbsp. coconut oil
- ½ tsp. vanilla (or 2 drops of Medicine Flower Vanilla)
- Optional: 1 tbsp. of raw almond butter

DIRECTIONS:

1. Blend kale and coconut milk first. Then add remaining ingredients and blend until smooth.

Savory Avocado Wrap

INGREDIENTS:

- 1 butter lettuce or collard leaf bunch
- ½ avocado
- 1 tsp. cilantro, chopped
- ¼ red onion, diced
- Small handful of spinach
- 1 tsp. chopped basil
- 1 tomato, sliced or chopped
- Sea salt & pepper

DIRECTIONS:

2. Spread the avocado on a collard leaf and then garnish it with basil, cilantro, red onion, salt and pepper, and tomatoes. Add

spinach if you want it to be a little fancier and then fold the leaf in half, so it is easier to handle and eat.
3. If you prefer the wrap with lettuce instead, repeat this procedure with lettuce instead.

Onion And Pepper Masala

INGREDIENTS:

- 1 large onion, chopped
- 1 bell pepper, chopped
- 2 garlic cloves, chopped
- 2 green chilis, chopped
- 1-inch ginger, grated
- 1 teaspoon cumin seeds
- ½ teaspoon turmeric powder
- 1 tablespoon cashews
- ¼ teaspoon asafetida
- 3 tablespoons tomato ketchup
- ½ teaspoon garam masala powder
- 1 teaspoon red chili powder
- Salt, to taste

- 1½ tablespoons vegetable oil

DIRECTIONS:

1. Heat 1 and a half tablespoons of oil in a non-stick pan and add cumin seeds, cashews, asafetida, turmeric powder, and sauté them until they are golden brown.
2. Add garlic, ginger, onion, and chilis until the onion becomes translucent and then add the salt. Adding the salt will make it cook faster, so be careful.
3. Add tomato puree or ketchup, garam Masala, and chili powder and then mix well. Add the bell peppers and some water as per desire and then cook for about five minutes until the bell pepper is cooked. Serve the dish hot.

Cauliflower Gnocchi

INGREDIENTS:

- 1 head of cauliflower
- steamed or boiled until very tender
- 1 cloves garlic, finely chopped
- 1 cup flour- of enough to make a soft dough
- 1 Tbs olive or coconut oil to fry
- 1 tin whole tomatoes
- 5 courgettis
- thickly sliced 1/2 onion
- finely sliced
- 1 Tbs olive or coconut oil
- 2 cloves garlic

- finely sliced 6 large black mushrooms, thickly sliced
- 300 ml vegetable stock
- 1 tsp sugar salt and pepper to taste
- fresh basil to serve

DIRECTIONS:

1. Blend the cauliflower and garlic until smooth. Add water if necessary and then smooth it into a paste. Add salt and flour and continue to blend them until you have dough ready. Add water if you need to make it more doughy if it is sticky.
2. Knead the dough until it is soft and then cut it into four pieces. Take one and cover the rest.
3. Roll the dough out and then cut into further smaller pieces as you keep progressing. Press each with a fork and

then repeat with the three pieces of dough remaining.
4. When ready, fry the gnocchi with some coconut or olive oil until it is golden on both sides.
5. When preparing ragout, put some oil in a pan and then heat it. Add garlic, onions, mushrooms, and courgettis and fry them until they are softening.

Add the vegetable stock and sugar, while reducing the flame. Season accordingly.

Serve ragout with warm cauliflower gnocchi, garnished with basil leaves.

Cole Slaw With Avocado Dressing

INGREDIENTS:

- ½ cup green or red cabbage 2 carrots

- 1 tomato

- 1 small red onion

- 3 tbsp. chopped parsley 1 avocado

- 3-4 tbsp. cold pressed extra virgin olive oil 1 fresh lemon, juice

- Dash of sea salt and cayenne pepper to taste

Directions:

1. 1.Shred cabbage and carrots, and finely chop the tomato, the onion and the parsley. Put in a big bowl.
2. 2.For the dressing, blend the avocado, the olive oil and the fresh lemon juice and

pour over the salad. Add salt and pepper to taste.

Fresh Garden Vegetable Salad

Ingredients:

- 1 head lettuce
- 2 tomatoes, chopped
- 2 carrots, shredded
- 1 red bell pepper(red green pepper), diced
  1 green bell pepper, diced
- 1 small cucumber, diced 1 red onion, thinly sliced

For the salad dressing:

- **1/3 cup fresh lemon and / or lime juice
  3/4 cup cold pressed olive oil**
- **1 tsp garlic powder**
- **½ tsp ground oregano**
- **¼ tsp dried rosemary 1 tsp dried basil**

- **½ tsp ground cumin**
- **1 dash of sea salt and cayenne pepper**

Directions:

1. 1.Put all vegetables in a big bowl and mix together. Pour the Salad Dressing over the salad and add some sea salt if required.
2. 2.Serve and enjoy!

Broccoli Salad With Tofu

Ingredients:

- 300g organic tofu
- 2 flowers of broccoli
- 5 tbsp. cold pressed olive oil 2 tbsp. soy sauce
- 1 tbsp. fresh lemon juice
- Some sea salt and pepper to taste 1 garlic clove
- ½ red pepper bell for garnishing

Directions

1. 1.Put diced tofu with some oil in a pan and fry for around 15 minutes. Turn off the stove, pour the soy sauce over the tofu and set aside.
2. 2.Now stir-fry the broccoli for 10 minutes. Also set aside to cool off.

3. 3.For the dressing, put the olive oil, the fresh lime juice, salt, pepper and the garlic in a blender and mix well until smooth. Then, put the tofu and the broccoli in a bowl, pour over the dressing and mix well. Garnish with slices of red pepper bell and finally - Enjoy your delicious alkaline salad!

Avocado Salad With Wild Garlic

INGREDIENTS:

- 1 avocado
- 1 bunch of wild garlic 3 tomatoes
- 1 red bell pepper
- 2 tbsp. of cold pressed extra virgin olive oil
  Some sea salt or organic salt to taste
- 1 pinch of cayenne pepper

DIRECTIONS:

1. 1.Cut the peeled avocado and the pepper bell first in half and then in thin slices. Chop the tomatoes in cubes and put everything in a medium-sized bowl.
2. 2.Then chop the wild garlic in very fine pieces and also put it into the bowl. Pour over the olive oil, mix well and taste with salt and pepper.

3. Finish! Enjoy your healthy alkaline salad!

Mediterranean Salad

Ingredients:

- 1 red bell pepper
- 1 yellow bell pepper 3 large tomatoes
- 10 black olives in oil 1 onion
- 1 small stalk of leek Some celery leaves
- For the salad dressing:
- 1/3 cup fresh lemon and / or lime juice 3/4 cup cold pressed olive oil
- 1 tsp garlic powder
- ½ tsp ground oregano
- ¼ tsp dried rosemary 1 tsp dried basil
- ½ tsp ground cumin
- 1 dash of sea salt and cayenne pepper

Diections

1. Dice the peppers and tomatoes and cut the onion, the leek and the celery leaves in very fine stripes. Then put all ingredients in a salad bowl.

Prepare The Salad Dressing:

2.Put all ingredients for the alkaline dressing in a blender and mix until all ingredients are well emulsified. Season again if desired. (If you prefer a thicker dressing, you can also add 1 tbsp. of flaxseeds before blending.)

3.Then pour the dressing over the veggies and mix well. Enjoy your healthy alkaline salad!

4.Many thanks to Marie from Germany for sharing this delicious alkaline recipe!

Quick & Easy Salad

INGREDIENTS:

- 2 ripe medium-sized avocados 8oz. carrots
- 8oz. broccoli
- 1/2 cup scallions 1 pinch of sea salt
- Your favorite fresh herbs

DIRECTIONS:

2. 1.Dice the avocados, chop the broccoli, scallions and herbs and shred the carrots. Put all veggies in a salad bowl, mix well and taste with salt.
3. 2.(Optional: you can add some flax seeds if you like). Enjoy this easy, quick & healthy salad!
4. Many thanks to Sam from Lewisville, Texas for sharing this delicious alkaline recipe!

Meal Recipe Plan

Ingredients:

- 12 an avocado
- Half a lemon, juiced
- 1 chopped and cored green apple
- Spinach, 1 cup
- Half a cucumber
- Coconut water, 1 cup

Directions:

3. All INGREDIENTS: should be smoothly combined.
4. As a hydrating and alkalizing breakfast smoothie.

Quinoa And Vegetable Stir

Ingredients:

- cooked quinoa, 1 cup
- 1 cup of mixed vegetables, including carrots, broccoli, bell peppers, and snap peas
- Olive oil, two tablespoons
- 1 tablespoon soy sauce or tamari
- 1 teaspoon of ginger, grated
- Sesame seeds, 1 teaspoon

Directions:

5. In a pan, heat the olive oil.
6. Ginger that has been grated should be included. till somewhat tender, stir-fry.
7. Add tamari and cooked quinoa. Mix thoroughly.
8. Sesame seeds can be added before serving.

Lentil Soup

Ingredients:

- 2 minced garlic cloves
- Six cups of vegetable stock
- Turmeric, 1 teaspoon
- 1/9 cup cumin
- Pepper and salt as desired
- Dried green lentils, 1 cup
- One sliced onion
- 2 sliced carrots
- 2 chopped celery stalks
- Garnishing with fresh parsley

Directions:

6. In a pot, sauté celery, carrots, and onion until tender.

7. Add the cumin, turmeric, and garlic. For one minute, cook.
8. Include vegetable broth and lentils. Till lentils are cooked, simmer.
9. Add salt and pepper to taste.
10. Before serving, garnish with fresh parsley.

Alkaline Spinach Salad

Ingredients:

- 1 sliced red bell pepper
- 1/4 of a thinly sliced red onion
- 30 grams of pumpkin seeds
- Tahini-lemon dressing
- 4 cups of young spinach
- Sliced cucumber, one

Directions:

5. Salad bowl with baby spinach in it.
6. Slices of red onion, red bell pepper, and cucumber should be placed on top.
7. Pumpkin seeds should be added to the salad.
8. Add a lemon-tahini dressing drizzle.

Alkaline Veggie Wrap

Ingredients:

- Sliced red bell pepper, half
- Sliced cucumbers, 1/4
- Sprouts (of broccoli or alfalfa)
- Pepper and salt as desired
- One whole-wheat wrap
- 50 ml of hummus
- 1 cup of mixed greens (arugula, kale, and spinach)
- Sliced avocado, half

Directions:
5. Wrapped in hummus, of course.
6. Add sprouts, red bell pepper, cucumber, avocado, and mixed greens on a plate.
7. Add salt and pepper to taste.
8. Cut the wrap in half after rolling it up.

Alkaline Roasted Vegetables,

Ingredients:

- 1 teaspoon dried oregano, thyme, and rosemary
- pepper and salt as desired
- 2 cups of mixed veggies, including carrots, bell peppers, cauliflower, and zucchini
- Olive oil, two tablespoons

Directions:

5. Set the oven's temperature to 400°F (200°C).
6. Combine olive oil, dried herbs, salt, and pepper with the mixed veggies.
7. Vegetables are spread out on a baking pan.
8. Roast for 20 to 25 minutes, or until vegetables are soft and gently browned.

Red Lentil And Kale Soup

Ingredients:

- 2 stalks of celery, chopped
- 1 bunch of kale, cut into ribbons
- 6 cups of vegetable broth
- 1 ½ cup red lentils, rinsed
- 1 tablespoon coconut oil
- 1 medium onion, finely chopped
- 4 garlic cloves, minced
- 2 large carrots, chopped
- Salt and pepper to taste

Directios:

4. Heat the oil in a large pot over medium heat. Add the onion and sauté until translucent – 3-5 minutes.

5. Add the garlic, carrots, celery and kale and sauté for 2-3 minutes. Add the broth, lentils, salt and pepper.
6. Cook on medium-low heat until lentils are tender, 20 minutesuinoa Stuffed Tomatoes

Quinoa

Ingredients:

- 1 can cannellini beans (i use eden organics, thoroughly rinsed and drained)
- 3 tbsp. Basil, julienned (thin strips)
- 2 tsp. Coconut oil
- 2 cups filtered water
- Sea salt (celtic grey sea salt, himalayan, or redmond real salt)
- 1 cup quinoa
- 4 medium tomatoes
- 3 cups baby spinach
- 2 cloves of garlic, minced
- Black pepper to taste

Directions:

9. Preheat oven to 375 degrees. Hollow out the tomatoes by cutting around the top of the tomato and scooping out the inside.
10. Slice a small section off the bottom of the tomato so it sits flat on the baking sheet. Sprinkle the inside of the tomatoes with some salt.
11. Cook quinoa by combining 2 cups of water with 1 cup of rinsed quinoa in a pot over high heat.
12. When the water comes to a boil, cover the pot and turn heat down to the lowest setting for 30 minutes.
13. Heat coconut oil in a pan, add garlic and brown lightly. Add beans, crush them slightly with a wooden spoon, and cook for one minute.
14. Add spinach and cook until wilted. Add basil. Season with sea salt and pepper.

15. Mix spinach mixture with quinoa. Divide the filling among the tomatoes. Place on a baking sheet lined with parchment paper.
16. Add a little water to the bottom of the baking sheet (4 tbsp. is plenty). Bake for 15-20 minutes at 375 degrees.

Blueberry Omega Morning Blast

Ingredients:

- 1 Tbsp. chia
- 1 Tbsp. ground flaxseed
- 1 Tbsp. hemp seed powder
- 1 Tbsp. coconut oil
- 1 cup coconut milk
- 1 large handful of spinach
- ½ cup blueberries
- 1 Tbsp. raw almond butter

Directions:

9. Preheat oven to 375 degrees. Hollow out the tomatoes by cutting around the top of the tomato and scooping out the inside.
10. Slice a small section off the bottom of the tomato so it sits flat on the baking sheet.

Sprinkle the inside of the tomatoes with some salt.
11. Cook quinoa by combining 2 cups of water with 1 cup of rinsed quinoa in a pot over high heat.
12. When the water comes to a boil, cover the pot and turn heat down to the lowest setting for 30 minutes.
13. Heat coconut oil in a pan, add garlic and brown lightly. Add beans, crush them slightly with a wooden spoon, and cook for one minute.
14. Add spinach and cook until wilted. Add basil. Season with sea salt and pepper.
15. Mix spinach mixture with quinoa. Divide the filling among the tomatoes. Place on a baking sheet lined with parchment paper.
16. Add a little water to the bottom of the baking sheet (4 tbsp. is plenty). Bake for 15-20 minutes at 375 degrees.

Cucumber Lavender Water.

Ingredients:

- 1 teaspoon dried lavender

- 1 small cucumber, thinly sliced

- 8 cups filtered water

Directions:

3. Combine all INGREDIENTS: in a pitcher and refrigerate for up to 12 hours to allow water to infuse.
4. Watermelon Mint Infused Water

Strawberry Quinoa Breakfast

INGREDIENTS:

- 2 tbsp. unsweetened shredded coconut flakes
- 5 tbsp. chia seeds
- 2 tbsp. almond pieces
- 1 cup cooked quinoa
- 2 pitted dates
- 1 ½ cup almond, coconut or hemp milk
- ½ cup quartered strawberries + 4 sliced strawberries

Directions:

5. Cook quinoa the night before and prepare the chia by blending almond milk with strawberries and 2 dates.
6. Blend until smooth, and then pour into a jar where you will add the chia seeds. Mix them as well as you can and then refrigerate.

7. Keep in mind that you need to put the lid on before refrigerating. In the morning before eating, place them all in a bowl and then add the quinoa and chia in.
8. Add almonds, strawberry slices, and shredded coconut.

Almond Butter Crunch Berry Smoothie

INGREDIENTS:

- 1 cup of any of the following (frozen mixed berries, strawberries or grapes)
- 1 tbsp. chia
- 4 tbsp. raw almond butter
- 2 cups fresh spinach
- 1 banana (peeled and frozen)
- 2 cups almond milk, unsweetened

Directions:

3. Blend in spinach with the almond milk. Add the remaining INGREDIENTS: in except the chia and then puree until smooth.
4. When it is smooth, add the chia and blend again at a very low speed. Let sit for a few minutes for the chia seeds to expand and then drink.

Quinoa Morning Porridge

INGREDIENTS:

- 1 tsp. chia seeds

- 1 tsp. hemp seeds

- ½ cup rinsed quinoa

- 1 15 oz. can of coconut milk

- 1 tsp. cinnamon

Directions:

3. Get all the INGREDIENTS: except hemp seeds and let them cook on the stove. Let them simmer for ten to fifteen minutes until all the liquid is absorbed.
4. When is it prepared, sprinkle it with hemp seeds to bring it all together as a very special little porridge.

Apple And Almond Butter Oats

Ingredients:

- 1/3 cup raw almond butter
- 1 tsp. cinnamon
- 1 cup grated green apple
- 1 ½ cups coconut milk
- 2 cups gluten-free oats

Directions:

4. Take the oats and put them in a bowl. Add in coconut milk and almond butter to mix them all together.
5. When they are mixed, cover the bowl with a lid or plastic wrap and refrigerate. You will need to leave this in the refrigerator overnight, so it is better to prepare it the last night.
6. If the oats get too thick, though, you may add some extra coconut milk to even it out.

Garnish it with cinnamon powder before eating.

Quinoa Burrito Bowl

Ingredients:

- 4 garlic cloves, minced
- 1 heaping tsp. cumin
- 2 avocados, sliced
- 2 limes, fresh juiced
- 1 cup quinoa (or brown rice)
- 4 green onions (scallions), sliced
- 2 15-oz cans of black or adzuki beans
- a small handful of cilantros, chopped

DIRECTIONS:

2. Cook the quinoa or rice (whichever you choose) with warm beans on a light flame. Stir it and add lime juice, onions, garlic, and cumin and then let the flavors

combine for ten to fifteen minutes. When the rice is finished, serve in separate bowls after being topped with beans, avocado, cilantro, and any other garnishing you may like.

Black Pepper To Taste

Ingredients:

- ½ cup kelp noodles, soaked and drained

- 1/3 cup cherry tomatoes, halved

- 2 tbsp. hemp seeds

- 3 cups kale, chopped

- ½ cup broccoli florets, chopped

- ½ zucchini (make noodles with a pasta roller)

Directions:

6. Flash steam the broccoli with kale for four minutes and then set it aside.
7. Mix the noodles you have rolled from zucchini and toss them with a serving of smoked avocado cumin dressing that you have prepared.
8. Add the cherry tomatoes and then toss the mixture. If preferred, drizzle the salad with

lemon tahini dressing and top it off with the dressed noodles.
9. Sprinkle the entire dish with hem seeds and enjoy.

Almond Butter And Banana Sandwich

Ingredients:

- 1 ripe banana, sliced
- Honey for drizzling
- 2 slices whole-grain bread
- 2 tablespoons almond butter

Directions:

7. Spread almond butter evenly on one slice of bread.
8. Lay banana slices on top of the almond butter.
9. Drizzle honey over the bananas if desired.
10. Top with the second slice of bread.
11. Press the sandwich together gently.
12. Slice in half diagonally if you prefer.

Alkaline Green Smoothie

Ingredients:

- 1 cup almond milk (alkaline)
- 1/2 lemon, juiced (alkaline)
- 1 teaspoon honey (acidic, use sparingly)
- 1 cup spinach (alkaline)
- 1 banana (alkaline)
- 1/2 avocado (alkaline)
- 1 tablespoon almond butter (alkaline)

Directions:

3. Blend all INGREDIENTS: until smooth.
4. Add honey if desired for sweetness (use sparingly).

Quinoa Salad With Chickpeas

Ingredients:

- 1/4 cup cherry tomatoes (alkaline)
- 1/4 cucumber (alkaline)
- 2 tablespoons olive oil (alkaline)
- 1 tablespoon lemon juice (alkaline)
- Salt and pepper to taste (use sparingly)
- 1 cup cooked quinoa (alkaline)
- 1/2 cup chickpeas (alkaline)
- 1 cup mixed greens (alkaline)

Directions:

5. In a large bowl, combine quinoa, chickpeas, mixed greens, cherry tomatoes, and cucumber.
6. In a separate bowl, whisk together olive oil and lemon juice.

7. Drizzle the dressing over the salad and toss to combine.
8. Season with salt and pepper to taste (use sparingly).

Baked Salmon With Steamed Asparagus

Ingredients:

- 1 clove garlic, minced (alkaline)
- Lemon wedges for garnish (alkaline)
- Salt and pepper to taste (use sparingly)
- 6-ounce salmon fillet (alkaline)
- 1 bunch asparagus spears (alkaline)
- 1 tablespoon olive oil (alkaline)

Directions:

8. Preheat the oven to 375°F (190°C).
9. Place the salmon fillet on a baking sheet lined with parchment paper.
10. In a small bowl, mix olive oil and minced garlic. Brush the mixture onto the salmon.
11. Season the salmon with salt and pepper to taste (use sparingly).
12. Arrange asparagus spears around the salmon.

13. Bake for 15-20 minutes or until the salmon flakes easily with a fork.
14. Serve with lemon wedges for garnish.

Green Salad With Avocado

Ingredients:

- ¼ cup red onion, thinly sliced
- ¼ cup feta cheese, crumbled
- 2 tablespoons olive oil
- 1 tablespoon lemon juice
- Salt and pepper to taste
- 4 cups mixed greens (lettuce, spinach, arugula, etc.)
- 1 ripe avocado, diced
- ¼ cup cherry tomatoes, halved
- ¼ cup cucumber, sliced

Directions:

6. In a large salad bowl, combine mixed greens, diced avocado, cherry tomatoes, cucumber, red onion, and crumbled feta cheese.

7. In a small bowl, whisk together olive oil, lemon juice, salt, and pepper to create the dressing.
8. Drizzle the dressing over the salad and gently toss to coat all INGREDIENTS: evenly.
9. Serve your Green Salad with Avocado as a light and refreshing side dish or add grilled chicken or shrimp for a complete meal.

Baked Salmon With Steamed Asparagus

Ingredients:

- 2 cloves garlic, minced
- 1 lemon, sliced
- Salt and pepper to taste
- Fresh dill for garnish
- 4 salmon fillets
- 1 bunch asparagus, trimmed
- 2 tablespoons olive oil

Directions:

1. Preheat the oven to 375°F (190°C).
2. Place the salmon fillets on a baking sheet lined with parchment paper.
3. Drizzle olive oil over the salmon, then sprinkle with minced garlic, salt, and pepper. Place lemon slices on top.

4. Bake for 15-20 minutes or until the salmon flakes easily with a fork.
5. While the salmon is baking, steam the asparagus until tender-crisp, about 5-7 minutes.
6. Serve the Baked Salmon with Steamed Asparagus, garnished with fresh dill and additional lemon slices if desired.

Sweet Potato And Chickpea Curry

Ingredients:

- 2 tablespoons curry powder
- 1 teaspoon ground cumin
- 1 teaspoon ground coriander
- ½ teaspoon ground turmeric
- Salt and pepper to taste
- Fresh cilantro for garnish
- 2 sweet potatoes, peeled and diced
- 1 can (15 oz) chickpeas, drained and rinsed
- 1 onion, chopped
- 2 cloves garlic, minced
- 1 can (15 oz) diced tomatoes
- 1 can (15 oz) coconut milk

Directions:

8. In a large pot, heat a bit of oil over medium heat. Add chopped onion and garlic, sauté until fragrant.
9. Add diced sweet potatoes and cook for a few minutes.
10. Stir in the curry powder, ground cumin, ground coriander, ground turmeric, salt, and pepper.
11. Pour in the diced tomatoes and coconut milk. Stir well.
12. Bring to a simmer, then cover and cook for 20-25 minutes, or until sweet potatoes are tender.
13. Add chickpeas and simmer for an additional 5 minutes.
14. Serve your Sweet Potato and Chickpea Curry hot, garnished with fresh cilantro. Enjoy with rice or naan bread.

Breakfast Smoothie

Ingredients:

- 1 tablespoon chia seeds
- 1 cup coconut water
- 1 teaspoon spirulina powder
- 1 tablespoon honey
- 1 cup spinach
- ½ cucumber
- ½ avocado
- 1 banana

Directions:

5. Place spinach, cucumber, avocado, banana, chia seeds, coconut water, and spirulina powder in a blender.
6. Blend until smooth.

7. Add honey for a touch of sweetness and blend again.
8. Pour into a glass and enjoy your nutritious Alkaline Breakfast Smoothie.

Grilled Lemon Herb Chicken

Ingredients:

- 2 tablespoons fresh rosemary, chopped
- 2 tablespoons fresh thyme, chopped
- Salt and pepper to taste
- 2 tablespoons olive oil
- 4 boneless, skinless chicken breasts
- 2 lemons, juiced and zested
- 2 cloves garlic, minced

Directions:

6. In a bowl, combine lemon juice, lemon zest, garlic, rosemary, thyme, salt, pepper, and olive oil to create a marinade.
7. Place chicken breasts in a resealable bag and pour the marinade over them. Seal the bag and refrigerate for at least 30 minutes.
8. Preheat the grill to medium-high heat.

9. Grill the chicken for about 6-8 minutes per side or until the internal temperature reaches 165°F (74°C).
10. Serve your Grilled Lemon Herb Chicken with your choice of sides.

Vanilla And Spelt Pancakes

Ingredients:

- 1 cup organic almond milk
- 1 tbsp maple syrup (you can also use alcohol-free stevia)
- 2 tbsp sunflower oil (cold and pressed)
- 11/2 tsp alcohol-free vanilla
- 1 cup light spelt flour (spelt is a non-wheat, whole grain flour)
- 2 tbsp aluminum-free baking powder
- 1/8 tsp fine grained Himalayan salt
- ¼ tsp coconut oil for the pan

Directions:

5. Mix all the dry and wet INGREDIENTS: into two different bowls. Hence, one bowl will have spelt flour, baking powder and

Himalayan salt while the other will have almond milk, sunflower oil and vanilla.

6. Mix the dry INGREDIENTS: and wet INGREDIENTS: separately and mix them together. Leave it aside for 10 minutes to allow the batter to rise. Use the coconut oil to grease the pan lightly.
7. Keep the pan on low heat and now spoon in small amounts of the batter. Allow it to cook for 2 to 3 minutes until bubbles appear on top. Then flip to cook the underside.
8. If you make extra pancakes, simply chill them in your refrigerator and pop them in the toaster the next day!

Green Breakfast Smoothie

Ingredients:

- 1 ripe avocado
- 1 cup coconut water
- Juice of one lime
- 1-2 tsp Udo's oil
- 1-2 tbsp hemp seeds
- One cucumber (about 6 ")
- 3 torn medium sized kale leaves
- 3 stems fresh parsley
- 5 stems fresh organic mint
- 1 " fresh ginger
- 2-3 drops Stevia

Directions:

2. Mix all the INGREDIENTS: in your blender until smooth and delicious! (You can add a little alkalized water if you like). If you prefer the natural sugars in the coconut, you can consider using almond milk instead.

Tropical Vegetable And Fruit Mix

Ingredients:

- A little salt to taste (about ½ tsp)
- 1 tbsp black strap molasses
- 4 1/4 cups organic milk
- 4 cups spelt flour
- ½ cup sesame seeds
- 2 tsp baking soda

Directions:

1. Preheat the oven to about 350 degrees Fahrenheit. Grease two 9 x 5 inch loaf baking pans.
2. Mix all the INGREDIENTS: together and pour the batter into the two pans. Bake the loaf for one hour or until the bread turns golden brown.

Pineapple And Coconut Smoothie

Ingredients:

- ½ cup coconut water
- 3 cups fresh pineapple
- 11/2 cups chopped spinach
- 11/2 cup organic almond milk
- 2 -3 tbsp unsweetened coconut flakes

Directions:

1. Mix everything together in your blender until smooth. Freeze the pineapple for an hour to make a cold, refreshing smoothie!

Additional Vegetables For Broth

Ingredients:

- 1 red onion, chopped
- ½ small cabbage
- ½ red pepper, diced
- 1 small zucchini
- 2 small carrots
- 2 ribs celery

Directions:

1. First, blend all the broth vegetables and set aside. Now steam-fry garlic and onions and add some filtered water and the broth.
2. Add in the carrots and squash and simmer for 4 minutes.
3. Now add in the celery and zucchini and simmer for 5 minutes.

4. Lastly, add in the tomatoes, cannellini beans and red peppers and simmer for 5 minutes more.
5. Sprinkle ½ -1 tsp Himalayan salt, basil and parsley after serving into bowls.

Sesame Flavored Broccoli Salad

Ingredients:

- 2 tbsp raw sesame oil
- 2 tbsp toasted sesame oil
- 4 cups chopped broccoli
- 2 tsp sesame seeds
- 1/2 tbsp Celtic sea salt

Directions:

1. Sauté and mix both sesame oils in a pan. Add in sesame seeds and add sesame seeds.
2. Gently stir and when it crackles, keep the oil and seed mixture aside. Bring a pot of filtered water to the boil and add in the chopped broccoli. Cook for 2 to 3 minutes.
3. Drain and place in a dish. Sprinkle the sesame seasoning and serve.

Sweet Potato And Lentil Bowl

Ingredients:

- 1 cup baby spinach

- 1/4 avocado, sliced

- 2 tablespoons pumpkin seeds

- 1 medium sweet potato, cubed

- 1/2 cup cooked green lentils

- Lemon-tahini dressing

Directions:

1. Steam or roast sweet potato cubes until tender.
2. Arrange baby spinach in a bowl.
3. Top with sweet potato, green lentils, avocado slices, and pumpkin seeds.
4. Drizzle with lemon-tahini dressing.

Alkaline Avocado And Cucumber Salad (Recipe 10)

Ingredients:

- 2 teaspoons chopped fresh dill
- Lemon juice from one
- Extra virgin olive oil drizzle
- 2 diced avocados
- Cuke, one, diced
- 1/4 red onion, chopped finely
- Pepper and salt as desired

Directions:

1. Avocado, cucumber, red onion, and chopped dill are all combined in a bowl.
2. Olive oil and lemon juice should be drizzled on.
3. Add salt and pepper to taste.
4. Gently stir by tossing.

Stuffed Bell Peppers

Ingredients:

- Chopped spinach, half a cup
- 14 cup finely minced red onion
- 14 cup finely minced fresh parsley
- Having the tops and seeds removed from four huge bell peppers
- cooked quinoa, 1 cup
- Diced tomatoes, 1 cup
- Tahini-lemon sauce

Directions:

1. Set the oven's temperature to 375°F (190°C).
2. Cooked quinoa, diced tomatoes, chopped spinach, red onion, and parsley should all be combined in a bowl.

3. Stuff the quinoa mixture inside each bell pepper.
4. The filled peppers should be put in a baking dish.
5. Add a glaze of lemon-tahini sauce.
6. Bake peppers for about 25 to 30 minutes, or until they are soft.

Pesto-Topped Alkaline Zucchini Noodles

Ingredients:

- Pine nuts, 14 cup
- Extra virgin olive oil, 1/4 cup
- one garlic clove
- lemon juice from one
- 2 spiralized zucchini for the noodles
- fresh basil leaves, 1/4 cup
- fresh parsley leaves, 1/4 cup
- pepper and salt as desired

Directions:

1. Combine basil, parsley, pine nuts, garlic, and lemon juice in a blender or food processor.
2. Olive oil should be added gradually while blending to achieve a smooth pesto.
3. Combine the pesto and zucchini noodles in a bowl.

4. Add salt and pepper to taste.

www.ingramcontent.com/pod-product-compliance
Lightning Source LLC
LaVergne TN
LVHW020437070526
838199LV00063B/4768